THE MANY FACETS OF A WOMAN

The Value of Friendships and Mentoring

SUZANNE HILLEGAS

Copyright © 2013 Suzanne Hillegas.

All rights reserved. No part of this book may be used or reproduced by any means, graphic, electronic, or mechanical, including photocopying, recording, taping or by any information storage retrieval system without the written permission of the publisher except in the case of brief quotations embodied in critical articles and reviews.

WestBow Press books may be ordered through booksellers or by contacting:

WestBow Press
A Division of Thomas Nelson
1663 Liberty Drive
Bloomington, IN 47403
www.westbowpress.com
1-(866) 928-1240

Because of the dynamic nature of the Internet, any web addresses or links contained in this book may have changed since publication and may no longer be valid. The views expressed in this work are solely those of the author and do not necessarily reflect the views of the publisher, and the publisher hereby disclaims any responsibility for them.

Any people depicted in stock imagery provided by Thinkstock are models, and such images are being used for illustrative purposes only.

Certain stock imagery © Thinkstock.

ISBN: 978-1-4497-9821-5 (sc)
ISBN: 978-1-4908-0253-4 (hc)
ISBN: 978-1-4908-0252-7 (e)

Library of Congress Control Number: 2013912975

Printed in the United States of America.

WestBow Press rev. date: 08/02/2013

Dedication

To my amazingly loving parents Gary and Diana Smith
who molded and crafted my creativity
and determination.

Foreword

By Rebekah Barbour

Suzy Smith Hillegas is one of my dearest friends. She is warm, kind, pleasant, organized, creative, courageous, artistic, confident; and though I could go on with my list, the thing that makes her so special is that she is a true friend. Not only does she choose her close friends with precision and purpose, she treats each one of them with that same care.

We first became close because she pursued our friendship in a time when I had nothing to give in return. She scheduled times for us to meet for coffee. She lent me the use of her house when I needed a quiet refuge to think and pray. She called for 10-minute conversations, just to keep in touch despite a busy season.

She has helped me celebrate some of my life's greatest accomplishments, and has walked beside me through my deepest valleys. We have laughed till we have made spectacles of ourselves, gulping in air and grabbing our aching sides. We have talked for hours, conversations lasting over several days, wrestling with the great mysteries of life: God, work, family . . . men. She has been brutally and beautifully honest when I could not see the truth or wanted to ignore it.

She reminds me of the disciple Andrew in the gospels. Every time he is mentioned, he is bringing someone to Jesus: his brother Peter, the boy with his lunch to be multiplied, and others that simply were curious about him. Suzy is like Andrew. The light inside of her, the joy she finds in her relationship with Jesus, is so contagious that I want to be with him too.

It is seen in every conversation I have with Suzy. Whether full of laughter or of tears, whether she is giving me good counsel or keeping me accountable, I walk away feeling closer to God than when we began. She is my Andrew, consistently taking me once again to the presence of My Savior.

That is not to say that everything has been all sunshine for Suzy. There have been times when life has dimmed her light and I wondered at the depth of the darkness to be able to quell the brightness of my friend. But she had her women. She had the strength of those of us that went to her, because she had come to us; those that picked up the phone at all hours day or night, because she had answered when we had called. Those relationships she had so carefully nurtured and developed, gathered around her proving strong enough to hold true till the light could shine again.

When we all came together at her wedding, I saw this amazing picture of God's family. People from all areas of one person's life, each with a different story, yet each so excited and so ready to celebrate such a happy day. This has to be how God designed His family to work all along.

This book is the family portrait up close. It is Suzy's family, her women, that have walked with her at different times along the journey. In it, you will see the sunshine, the darkness, the laughter, and the tears. You will see how God moves in his people. You will see Jesus and Suzy will bring you to him.

I am honored to be included in her book, but so much more, I have the pleasure of being in her circle of women and to call her my friend.

Table of Contents

Introduction xiii

Chapter 1: Determined Diana 1

Chapter 2: Parenting Pam 11

Chapter 3: Thought-Full Tracy 21

Chapter 4: Inviting Iris 27

Chapter 5: Adventuresome Addie 33

Chapter 6: Mirror Mira 39

Chapter 7: Precisely Private Vivian 47

Chapter 8: Prayer Warrior Wendy 55

Chapter 9: Grief and Gratitude Gretchen 61

Chapter 10: Fast Friends Felicity and Faith 69

Chapter 11: Lover of Souls Sophie 75

Chapter 12: Mentoring Towards God, Towards Hope 81

INTRODUCTION

There is a scene in the middle of the movie *27 Dresses* when the two sisters are finally having it out. They are each saying all the things that she believed the other woman thought of her all their lives. At the beginning of the fight they are yelling out these comments and then, as the absurdity of what one sister is saying to the other becomes evident, they begin to calm down. The conversation takes a more honest and personal turn. The older, more stable, sister sees her younger, freer sister as happier and luckier. The younger sister sees her settled sister's life as the life she would like to have. Near the end of this revealing conversation the younger sister says, "I was trying to be you." And the older sister responds with "Why? Why would you want to be me, when you get to be you?"[1]

This is the cry of all women. We look at other women and think *I just want to have her body* or *I just want to have her ease in the middle of a crowd*. We struggle to be satisfied with what we have and, more importantly, who we are as women.

---

[1] Anne Fletcher, Director. 2008. *27 Dresses* [Motion Picture]. USA: Fox 2000 Pictures.

How can this deep-rooted habit of wishing to be someone else be flipped around to be a positive help instead of detrimental disease? Mentoring. Choose a mentor, be a mentor, invade women's lives to learn from them and grow. Find the traits that you have always longed for and discover that you have something to offer as well. We as women have so many facets. We are multi-dimensional. I set out to learn as much as I could from very specific women. Sometimes a relationship was thrust upon me, often I requested it.

Having a woman mentor can help you see things about yourself that you did not even know were there. Mentoring creates a space to be not-okay and to examine why you are heading down a particular path. The truths and characteristics that you can learn from another woman are invaluable. For many years I thought I was the one taking. I had no idea I was also giving in these friendships. These women had much more experience and life understanding than I thought I ever would have. But as the years have gone by, I see that being part of a mentorship is not a taking but a sharing: a sharing of lives, a sharing of failures, and a sharing of hope. Hope of becoming a more authentic, lovelier, stronger woman than I was before the friendship began.

Many women have been hurt by female friendships and thus retreat, choosing not to be vulnerable to other women in the future. Those hurts are real and painful, and f you have been hurt you are not alone, but I hope you will think about finding a mentor. God designed women to need each other, to talk together, to smile together, to realize we are not alone in our struggles and our fears. But mostly we need to cry and laugh together. Often in my loneliest times it was the women in my life that brought me healing, hope and a safe place to lay my burdens. If you are a woman who has been hurt by other women, I am sorry. But the world is filled with countless other women and many of them could be a healing balm to your wounded soul. I hope that after reading about the lovely women in my life you will be brave and try one more time. You will find the blessed peace in having a friend that you can call in the middle of the night to cry with, or stop by her house or workplace in the middle of the day to tell her that you got the job or that you are getting married or that you finally found the right sweater on sale and bought it.

The women in my life have made me who I am today. I do not know where I would be without them. After years of having mentors and being a mentor, I can almost immediately tell when I have met a friend for life. Because I value my friendships so much, I will be changing the names of these women and the places where we met. I hope that as they read this book they will recognize themselves. I want to share the intimacy of our friendships but not their private lives. They have trusted me with their stories and their hearts, and I want to honor that. I have chosen names that make for great alliterations. One of my hopes is that you will go along, recognizing whom these women represent in your own life.

A woman has many facets. Facet is derived from a French word, facette, which means face.[2] The many faces of a woman. We were designed as multi-dimensional beings. Remember Mary: God knew she needed a companion, a woman to accompany her through the interesting process of becoming a

---

[2] www.merriam-webster.com/dictionary/facet

mother. The fact that he chose a woman beyond child-bearing years to be that companion is lovely. Elizabeth already had much life experience that she could share with Mary. Elizabeth had probably discovered many of her own different facets, yet now here was a new one: motherhood, which she had longed for for a very long time. I find it fascinating that the angel encouraged Mary to go to Elizabeth. They were so different. Their lives were dissimilar, yet they found comfort in each other. They each found comfort where she was in life.

As I take you through the different mentoring relationships that have shaped me and formed me into the woman I am today, I would ask you to think about several things. Have you had a friendship like this one? Did you view yourself on the receiving end or on the giving end? As your life changes and evolves, have your friendships evolved as well? Have you made it a point to make any new friends this year?

The most important question of all: Is mentoring truly an extraordinary experience? Let's read and find out.

Chapter 1

Determined Diana

The Merriam-Webster Dictionary defines determination as "the act of deciding definitely and firmly, also, the result of such an act of decision; firm or fixed intention to achieve a desired end." What comes to your mind when you hear words like definitely and firmly? I think of my mom, Diana D. Smith. Determination could have been her middle name. It was actually Davis, but still she was the most determined woman I have ever met and she demonstrated it to me every day of her life.

The first five years of a child's life are the most formative. Studies have shown that sleep patterns are established, eating habits are established, and language is decoded and implemented. These patterns and skills are the foundation of who we are. Mentoring as a skill or trait—I am not sure how to define it—was modeled for me from the moment I entered the world. My mother introduced me to the concept by modeling it for me. She delighted in who I was, helped to shape my character, and demonstrated traits to me that I would not naturally possess.

Diana Smith and I were two very different people. She was strong, steady, and sure of herself. My brothers and I have discussed how and when we each learned not to mess with Mom. What she said was what she meant. If she told us that we were only going to get one warning before a consequence, then we only got one warning. I cannot single out an event when I suddenly knew Mom always did what she said, that was just how it had always been.

Diana Smith was steady. Her faith, her family, and her friends were her highest priorities. Some would describe her as stubborn but most would describe her as steady and competent. When there was a topic that she wanted to understand, she would educate herself through books and literature. She was an avid reader and could answer almost any *Jeopardy!* question.

Confidence was one of her greatest assets. Mom was not arrogant, but sure of herself. She knew her gifts and strengths and was always ready to use them. But she also knew her weaknesses and would often choose to focus on her strengths.

When I was six months old, my mother noticed that something was not quite right with her lovely new little girl. Her eyes were different from those of the two boys she had already been blessed with. In her motherly, steadfast strength, she began taking me to doctors. One doctor told her I would never live a normal life. She was not satisfied with this diagnosis, and made another appointment with a different doctor. After several appointments and opinions she finally found one that would offer us both hope. And the journey of opening my eyes began.

For a year and a half, my mom frequently drove an infant, who grew into a toddler, to the eye specialist located two hours away. It was determined that I should be fitted for a pair of glasses at the age of two. I do not remember this process but one of my earliest memories is of that day. I think it stands out so clearly in my mind because I could not see and then suddenly I could. My mom loved to tell the story of the day I was gifted better sight.

We lived in a small rural town in the mountains of California. We had to drive over a mountain range and down into the San Bernardino Valley to see the eye doctor. Forty years ago it was not common for very young children to have glasses. We went for the appointment. I received my glasses, and the whole world was opened up to me. As we walked out of the big building where the doctor's office was located it was a clear, beautiful day. The vistas extended for miles in every direction. As we stepped out of the building and into the sun, I reached out my hand to the mountains that were many miles away. I looked up at my mom and said, "I touch the mountains!"

Tears welled up in my strong, steadfast mother's eyes, and she said, "Yes, you can touch the mountains."

This was the gift my mother gave me throughout her life, the ability to touch and climb over mountains, actually life-hurdles that often feel like mountains. She demonstrated the determination and strength I often lacked.

Mom was determined to make my life as normal as possible. She wanted me to have every opportunity that a 20/20-vision kid could have. I went to school, I made friends,

I learned to love reading just like my mom. I would devour books (depending on the print size).

My brothers and I attended a small Christian school. We memorized verses and had Bible class every day. Bible print is often very, very small. I really struggled to read the necessary texts for different assignments. Mom, ever-resourceful, found me a large-print Bible (which, again, was rare so many years ago). This book was enormous. I remember having to keep my desk really clean so all of my books could still fit inside the desk. I never wanted to be different from the other kids, but I also wanted to do well in school. Mom was always seeking out ways to normalize my life.

The character of Diana Smith was steadfast, strong, and determined. "The buck stops here" was very much a phrase my brothers and I used to describe Mom. She was a steady disciplinarian. Wisdom and dedication were the traits that many women admired about my mom. She loved to laugh. Often her friends would come to her and ask for her advice about marriage, family, and life. The level of honesty that spilled forth from her at times could be overwhelming, but we always knew she genuinely cared about us and that she was telling us the absolute truth.

An event that occurred when I was 20 absolutely demonstrates my mom's level of steadiness and strength. It has been 18 years since I had tried to touch the mountains. The first doctor had been wrong; I had had a very normal life. I had learned to play the piano, I had graduated from high school, and was currently enrolled for my senior year of college in South Carolina. But my eyes were continuing to be the thing that molded my character and life. I had to have an eye surgery where healthy tissue was removed from my left eye and sewn over the unhealthy tissue in my right eye. I had had three other surgeries, but they had been outpatient, and minimal compared to this one.

A series of events was about to unfold that will forever be burned into my mind. My mother loved to be overly prepared for everything. She had gotten my pain prescription ahead of time so that after the surgery I could immediately start taking it. The doctor had told us that I would feel like I had rocks in my eyes for several days.

We arrived to the hospital, checked in, got me into the gown that does not close in the back, and waited. I was very nervous. Mom, knowing I needed a distraction, tried to find a TV channel we could watch but all the stations were swamped with the O. J. Simpson trial. We waited and we waited. Mom kept complaining of a headache. She finally decided to take something. She was like a walking medicine cabinet. She used an old prescription bottle to carry all of her "medicine" around. She found what she was looking for, borrowed my water glass and swallowed the pill. About five minutes later she said, "Oh, no." My mother never said "Oh, no," especially not on important days like this.

"What, Mom?"

She replied, ever so calmly, "I think I just swallowed one of your Vicodin." Mom would become violently ill in reaction to Vicodin. She said, "I should stick my finger down my throat to make myself throw up. But I won't. Everything will be fine."

I had a very bad feeling about this. Mom never said stuff like that. Sure enough, within five minutes she was in the little curtained bathroom of my room, violently ill. I was in shock. There was nothing I could do. My mom sat down beside me. I asked how long she thought it would last and she guessed about 12 hours. 12 hours! My surgery was only supposed to be three hours.

Finally it was my turn to be rolled away. Apparently while I was gone, Mom lay in my hospital bed and tried to rest. After about an hour of throwing up there was nothing left in her stomach so she was able to rest miserably.

The surgery was fine and all went as planned. While I was in post-ops the doctor went to inform my mom about the surgery. Apparently I needed drops put in my eyes every few hours to keep infection from setting in. The doctor stressed how important these drops were. Mom dragged herself out of my bed and went to find the pharmacy to get the drops prescription filled. She was about to test her steadiness and her strength. The pharmacy was on the other side of the campus; the campus was over six blocks long. Mom told me later that she prayed every step of the way. "God, my daughter needs me and I think I might pass out. Please get me there and back safely."

She did return to my room where I was all bandaged up and trying to drink some apple juice. I had to drink the whole cup before I could leave the hospital. Mom was desperate to get us to the hotel so we both could lie down and rest. It took me forever to drink that apple juice. But finally it was gone.

My dad was the chauffeur. He brought the car around and loaded in his two miserable patients. When we finally got up to our hotel room, the drapes drawn, Mom and I each took a bed, Dad was sent away somewhere, and we rested and rested and rested. At some point later in the evening I requested a shake from McDonald's. I heard Mom pipe up that she would like one, too. Dad was tremendously glad to have something to do; he zipped out the door to make our request a reality.

In the middle of the night I had to get up and use the bathroom. This was a real chore as I could not see and each time I sat up blood would rush to my eyes. It was quite painful. Mom was feeling better by this point and Dad was snoring away, relieved to have made it through this incredibly stressful day. Mom helped me to the bathroom. When I was seated on the bed again I said I was hungry. Mom cut up an apple for me. Laughter is one of the greatest treasures you can share with someone. My mom and I shared much of it. But this day had had none. As Mom was slicing me the apple she said, "You know if I had been feeling better today in the hospital I would have taken your apple juice and flushed it down the toilet, then we could have left an hour sooner." This tickled me so much I started to giggle. Giggling is infectious. Mom began to giggle and then she began impersonating the nurse. "You drink your juice, Susane, and then you can go home! You need to go home, your momma is very sick, drink your juice, Susane!" We got laughing so hard that my eyes began to water, which stung terribly. We quickly had to try to stop but we just couldn't help it. We kept impersonating the nurse. We were each so relieved that the other was okay and well.

As the years went by this became our favorite story to tell. We always would crumble into laughter because of the absolute ridiculousness of it all.

Her steady determination was linked to confidence. At first, this seemed to conflict with my natural impulse to please people. It is important to me that the emotional energy in the room is calm and in harmony. As a result of this desire, often I will not stand up for myself. I do not want to be the one that tips the scale. My mom demonstrated to me and for me how and why to stand up for myself. One of her classic sayings was, "If you don't stand up for yourself, nobody else is going to do it for you."

Because of my mom, I have much more confidence than I would have had on my own. She mentored me through countless difficult situations. I often wanted to feel sorry for myself or let the circumstances of my life defeat me. She would have none of that. We would revisit topics, teachers, and temperaments until she felt I was ready to have a better attitude or more confidence in the situation.

But one of the very best things about Diana Smith was her pragmatism. She was the queen of practicality. Often, as a child, this was quite upsetting to me because I wanted to do the thing that was fun or impulsive, not practical. But as an adult it has proven to be a wonderful attribute. I lean more to the creative side of life myself, but because my mother was willing to mentor me and teach me the value of practicality, this is a trait that others often most admire in me. In almost any situation I can figure out what my mother's advice would be. Whatever is the most practical choice is what she would recommend.

Last but not least is the lesson that family comes first. What I learned from my mom is I can do whatever it is I have to do for my family. It does not matter how awful I feel or how daunting the task. If someone needs me, I figure out how to help them and get it done. I am so grateful I had so many years of my mom demonstrating these traits to me, over and over again.

Chapter 2

Parenting Pam

I had always heard that motherhood was a joy, but it seemed that there were not any mothers who were enjoying it. At this time I was working in a day care center, taking care of toddlers. It was a challenging and physically draining job. There is no way I could have done this job and had children of my own. Interacting with children all day and then their parents really gave me an education in the life of the stressed-out parent.

The parents I observed varied vastly. There were calm parents. No matter how their day at work had been or what their child's report for the day was, they were calm and agreeable and ready to listen. Then there were the continuously stressed-out parents. They were always in a hurry, they never had time to enjoy their child or hear a good report of their child. They wanted the facts and only facts as quickly as possible. If we could have had their child packed up and ready to be whisked from the window as they drove by, that may have put smiles on their faces. These were two extreme types of parents; another was the parents who could be utterly manipulated by their child. As soon as the manipulated parent walked through the door the child would start crying or whining or running or just being difficult. I was always shocked by this as I had spent all day with the child, who had readily obeyed and been quite pleasant. Some of these kids couldn't even talk yet, but they already knew how to push their parents' buttons.

The parents who walked in, greeted their child, greeted me, and offered everyone some room to breathe were my favorite type. If the child wanted to show them something in the classroom they would go look. There was a rhythm and routine to what they did with their child. The child knew the boundaries and often stayed within them. If, on a particular day, the child was being overly obstinate the parent would go through the routine: hugging the child, checking the diaper bag, picking up the cup, and collecting any other miscellaneous items. The parent was not controlled by the child's behavior. These parents were always refreshing to me and my staff. I fervently wanted to learn how to be this type of a parent.

I began my search: where was a woman that I could learn from, that could mentor me and show me how to enjoy the children in my life? I found her. Parenting Pam will be her nickname. She had three children between the ages of three and eight when I first met her. Her family attended the same church as I did and she worked at the same university. How do you walk up to someone and say, "I love the way that you parent and want to learn; will you please teach me?" It felt too direct. So I came up with an alternative way to get in the door. At church a couples retreat was coming up. Many people knew what I did for a living and I knew several would ask me to watch their children during the retreat. I decided to be proactive. One day as we were all eating in the U cafeteria, I volunteered my services to Parenting Pam and her husband Pete. They were quite surprised. They said that they had just started talking about it and realized they needed to ask someone soon to watch their children. They were overjoyed that I had volunteered. They invited me over for dinner so that I could get to know the kids better and acquaint myself with the culture of their family.

At times we make very small decisions in our lives that lead to amazing things. We don't know it at the time, nor do the people we are interacting with. My life was about to change forever. The ways I viewed marriage, parenting, and being a woman were all about to shift, and none of us knew it. At five o'clock, I arrived at their house and was pleasantly greeted by everyone in the household. As I stepped into their home I felt like I stepped into a whole new dimension. The house was simple, but tasteful. The children showed off their "clean" bedrooms. Then I was taken outside to see the garden and swing set. As I was escorted back into the house it was time for dinner. They had only one bathroom, so we all took turns washing our hands. We sat down to the table and the meal began.

Parenting Pete prayed for the meal, and then the food was passed around. Everyone was very polite and well behaved at the table. I thought, "It's because I am a visitor and they want to impress me." In actuality, this was the normal expectation of this peaceful household.

After having a great time with the kids while their parents were away at the couples retreat, a lovely new friendship began with each member of the household, not just Parenting Pam. We shared many more meals at the large farm-style table. During one meal Pete was away. Before the meal began, Parenting Pam asked if we needed anything else on the table. Everyone looked around and it seemed that we had everything. We all sat down, Pam blessed the food and eating commenced. About ten minutes into the meal the middle daughter jumped out of her chair to get some juice out of the refrigerator. As she was standing at the refrigerator door, her mother said her name: "Patricia."

The daughter looked up and some sort of recognition came across her face. She immediately put the juice back in the fridge, sat down, and said, "Sorry, Mama."

Parenting Pam looked her in the eye and calmly said, "You are finished with your meal, please take your plate to the sink." Patricia obeyed and then retreated to her room. As I looked around the table the other two children were quietly eating their food, as was Pam. It was like nothing had happened. I stared at Pam, she smiled and winked at me. I kept eating but had so many questions flitting through my mind. What just happened? Why was she dismissed from the table? Does this happen often?

A few minutes later Parenting Pam excused herself from the table. She carried her plate to the sink, she turned to all of us and said, "When you are finished with your meal, you may be excused from the table. Please put your plate in the sink and help clean up the kitchen." The children responded with, "Yes, Mama," and pursued clearing their plates.

As soon as Pam was out of the room I could not contain myself any longer. I asked the kids, "What just happened?"

The Many Facets of a Woman

They both calmly looked at me and the older one said, "Patricia disobeyed Mama."

And then the younger one said, "Mama is talking to her in her room right now, they will be out soon. Could I take your plate to the sink for you?" I stammered out a yes and decided to hold my questions for Pam.

Sure enough mother and daughter returned and all seemed right in the household again. The kitchen found a level a cleanliness that satisfied the mother and the children were sent outside to play. As soon as the kids were outside Parenting Pam turned to me and said, "I will gladly explain what happened at dinner." I had not even gotten the question out of my mouth.

As we sat in the front room Pam began to explain her philosophy of parenting. She believed that children should obey right away with a good response and with respect. She also strongly believed in rewarding positive behavior and disciplining negative behavior.

She explained that earlier in the week the family had been having dinner together. It seemed that every two or three minutes someone was jumping up to get something, go to bathroom, or do something else. Her husband said that this would end that night. Beginning at the next meal, anyone who got up from the table before they were excused would not be finishing the meal. Pam explained that sure enough, because all of them were out of practice, one of the children had gotten up without permission and Pete had followed through with the consequence of immediately ending the meal for that child. Since the first night none of them had broken the rule, until tonight. Even though Pete was not there it was important, Pam explained, for her to follow through with the standard he had set. I suggested that maybe Patricia had forgotten. Pam's response was kind and firm. She said, "But I want to raise a daughter who remembers and who doesn't make excuses for herself." And here I was seeing it play out in real life.

I asked Pam, "Did you feel bad about not letting her finish her meal?"

Pam thought for a moment and then responded with, "That is neither here nor there. The point is that Patricia will not starve and she will think twice the next time she wants to jump up from the table to get something." All I could think while I sat there was that I have so much more to learn.

Because Pam delighted in her children, they in turn delighted in her. She had a very special relationship with each child. She relished in rewarding them for positive behavior. Sometimes the reward was small, like staying up late on a Friday night or receiving words of affirmation. Sometimes the reward was large like going on a fishing trip with just their dad or having several friends over for a sleepover. Many times the reward was living in a peaceful household; knowing the boundaries of life, knowing that each member would be treated fairly, and knowing that unconditional love was always present and readily given.

I became a regular fixture at the P. household. We all had such a good time together that any spare time I had I spent at their place. On a particular Saturday morning another significant incident happened. Pete was at work and the two older girls were visiting at a friend's house, so just Pam, her son Petee, and I were together. Around 11:00 a.m. we had decided we would head over to the U cafeteria to get lunch. Petee had been busy all morning building and planning as only a 5-year-old boy can. Pam called him into the room, explained the plan for lunch, and then asked him to go put on his shoes so that we would all be ready to go. He replied with the consistent, "Yes, Mama" and left the room. Several minutes went by and Petee came racing back into the room. He had a rope in one hand and a dinosaur in the other and no shoes on his feet. "Mama, can you help me tie up this dinosaur?"

Pam looked him right in the eye and said, "No, I cannot help you with that right now. But I would like you to go to your room and wait for me." This was code for: you are in trouble and I will be in shortly to give you discipline for your actions. Pam excused herself from me and followed her son. As I was flipping through a magazine I heard Petee cry, which meant he had received a spanking. A few more quiet moments passed and both mother and son returned, ready to leave for lunch.

After lunch Petee ran off to play at a nearby tree and I had some questions. Why had he gotten a spanking for not putting on his shoes? I thought all kids forgot to put on their shoes. Again Pam graciously reminded me of her philosophy. Children should obey right away with a good response and with respect. Pam also shared that she realized she had not been consistent lately with following through. She had asked Petee to forgive her for not being consistent and told him that she would be more consistent in the future. As we watched Petee play with the other children Pam said, "Honestly I didn't want to spank him today, but it is more important to be consistent as a parent than to do what I want to do."

Then as if on cue a parent came out of the cafeteria, called to her son to come as it was time to go, and the child responded with a loud "NO!" and ran the other way. The parent then called louder, the child just retorted louder. The frustrated parent began throwing out threats: "If you don't come right now, then . . ." The child did not even look up from where he was playing at this point.

We also needed to leave and pick up the older girls. Pam called out, "Petee, it is time to go, please come." He immediately looked up, called out "Yes, Mama," said good bye to his friends and ran over to where we were standing. As the three of us walked away hand in hand I looked back to see the yelling parent was now chasing the child around the tree trying to catch him. Parenting Pam winked at me over Petee's head and smiled. She was right, it is worth the time and effort to train your children to obey right away with a good response and with respect, no matter what the request. Parenting really could be a joy, or not, as was so clearly illustrated in the sunlight around a tree.

It has been many years since that day under the tree. Pam affected my life in more ways than I realized at the time. She lived her life honestly and willingly in front of others. She cared deeply about our friendship. I often felt I was being a bother or asking too much. Pam would always put my anxiety to rest. She enjoyed the friendship and wanted it. She would challenge me as well. It was quite common for Pam to look into my life and speak truth about situations I was dealing with. She expected the same honesty from me that she offered to me every day. There are times even now so many years later, when I will stop and think through an old conversation I had with Pam: What would be her advice? What honest question would she ask me? She taught me how to be honest about myself and how to offer that same honesty to others. Parenting Pam's friendship was a privileged one indeed.

CHAPTER 3

THOUGHT-FULL TRACY

What is the most thoughtful thing that has ever been said to you? Who said it to you? As I have observed people, I've noted that thoughtfulness is often very well thought out. The thoughts of a caring person are full of other people and their needs. How does one learn to become more thought-full? What is the secret? I think one of the key elements is observation. Observe thoughtful people whenever you encounter them. Another element is doing something. So often people have a good idea about how to help someone but then time whizzes by and no action is ever taken. I think being a thought-full person is being an action-oriented person. Thought-Full Tracy was just such a person.

The Bible encourages us to find older, wiser women to spend time with. Sometimes the woman who is wiser is standing right in front of us, sometimes we have to seek her out, and sometimes she seeks us out. I was young and swamped. Thankfully, Tracy could see needs often before they even occurred. Tracy was a woman such that, even as we were becoming friends, I did not realize she was a woman of wisdom who wanted to help me. She interacted with me every day, and was always quick with encouragements and positive insights and verses of Scripture.

Tracy and I crossed paths during my first teaching job. I was working at a small Christian school in Northern California. I was fulfilling my dream of being a teacher. I was assigned 19 first graders and was expected to teach them something—no, actually many things—by June of the following year. I remember standing on the playground the first day of school and thinking, "I am in charge of these kids, no one else but me." I think it was a low level of panic that rippled through my body.

The first week I was there Tracy invited me over for dinner. Present at dinner were Tracy, her husband, I and another member of the staff, Tammy. Tammy and I hit it off great and became fast friends. I found out several months later that it had been Tracy's plan to connect Tammy and me. She thought I would need a friend and she was so right.

I benefitted again from Tracy's thoughtfulness and ingenuity several weeks after the school year had begun. A staff meeting had just ended. One item from the meeting agenda was the importance of completing the textbooks. Another item was being ready to do first quarter report cards. I was so overwhelmed. I had no idea how I was going to accomplish either of those tasks. As everyone left the room I just sat at the table. Tracy was the school librarian and assisted with reading. Despair must have been plastered across my face. She sat down next to me.

She began the conversation with, "That is a lot to take in, isn't it?" I realized I had been sitting there in a haze and I just nodded mutely. Tracy continued, "Which item from the meeting are you struggling with the most?"

I burst into tears. "All of it!" I stammered out.

Tracy always made this great facial expression of thought. As we sat there staring at each other, tears trickled down my cheeks. Tracy began to ask very simple questions about my classroom and the students that I had. I was able to answer these questions but I was thinking, "How is this information going to help anything?" She continued to ask and I continued to answer. As Tracy's gentle questions got my emotions down off of the ledge, I was able to think a little more clearly and express the issues that were really bothering me.

The first was the teaching manuals I was carrying home every night to prepare for the next day. But I had hurt my back earlier in the summer. Carrying the huge books back and forth only aggravated my back. The second issue was grading. I was trying to grade every piece of paper my students did. Do I make things worth 2 points, 12 points, or 200 points? I just wasn't really sure. I am a very precise person. I like to know what is expected and then I like to exceed the expectation. But I had set the expectation too high. I couldn't reach it. I was failing and very soon everyone was going to see!

Tracy continued to talk with me, to encourage me, and, most importantly, to help me find solutions. We tackled the grading piece first. She had been a teacher several years before becoming the librarian and she shared what she used to do and then what the teacher after her did. She came up with a way to reorganize the students' work and my work so that I knew which papers should be graded and which papers were just used for review. Two hours later, dry-eyed and with a newly acquired ally, I was ready to jump back into the trenches of being a first year teacher.

A week after this highly emotional meeting, Tracy showed up at my classroom door with several book bags. She had taken all of my teaching manuals to a print shop to unbind them and punch holes in the side of each page. I couldn't understand it, why had she done this? She smiled at me and said, "This way you don't have to take home the whole manual. You can take out the pages you need, put them in one notebook, and then you only have one book in your bag instead of five!" I couldn't even process it. It was so thoughtful and so practical. And it worked. It saved my back and it made sense to my very scattered brain.

As the year went by, Tracy and I developed a lovely friendship. She would check in on me occasionally. We both liked to scrapbook and we would go to a special scrapbooking store on Saturdays and just get lost in creativity and photos.

During this year I lived with a very difficult roommate. The roommate also worked at the same school. Most of the staff didn't deal with her at all, but because we were roommates, I was often aware of the tension she caused when she was in the room. In the spring Tracy and her husband were taking a three-week trip overseas. One afternoon Tracy asked if I would be interested in house sitting while she and her husband traveled. I leaped at the opportunity. Tracy had made sure the kitchen was well-stocked. There were stacks of books I could read, movies I could watch, and I had access to every room in the house.

I did not realize how much I needed a break, but Tracy did. Those three weeks were exactly what I needed to get me to the end of the school year. After she returned we spent a Saturday together and we talked about all the blessings I had received from staying at her house, the main one being a reprieve from my roommate. Tracy shared with me all the traits that she admired in me. She told me how proud she was of me and was amazed at how well I had done throughout the year.

This meant so much to me. I had the highest regard for Tracy and often felt very inferior in the friendship. But she had received blessings from helping me and sharing her wisdom and practical ideas. Tracy demonstrated for me that we can be passionate, fun, and excellent in whatever we do. It is worth wrestling through the hard issues to find a solution. I never felt judged by her. She was always so gracious and helpful to me, and I so desire to cultivate that trait in my own life.

As many years have gone by I look back on that very first year of teaching and just have to smile. I was reckless, naive, and much too perfectionistic to survive. Tracy was a lovely balance to those traits with her spirit of fun, her wonderful wisdom, and her grace to help me realize I could not reach all my goals at once. I am grateful to her and for her. She taught me many things by just being comfortable in her own skin and life.

It is important to be willing to share your life. Mentoring is about sharing. In this day and age it is so easy to compartmentalize people. This group of people is my work friends. On the weekends I have my adventuresome friends and my church friends. Tracy taught me that a good friend mixes up the compartments. But it is so great when the

Suzanne Hillegas

compartmental lines are crossed and you can enjoy several different layers of friendship with someone else. Thought-Full Tracy definitely gave me many full thoughts to ponder in the loveliness of our friendship.

Chapter 4

Inviting Iris

I am always excited when an invitation arrives in the mail. It could be an invitation to anything: boating on the lake, a birthday party, a 50th wedding anniversary, or a Super Bowl Party, and I will be excited. An invitation speaks of intentionality and specialness. An invitation implies that I am wanted and expected for a specific event. My name was on a list, and I was sent an invitation. How do I translate that same excitement and intentionality into friendship?

Sometimes we invite people into our world, but sometimes we are thrust into others' worlds. It was important to me to learn how to be inviting. Bluntness can often be my loudest trait, and I wanted to learn how to curb my bluntness with graciousness. Family is such an interesting place to gain a mentor. But thankfully I have two brothers and, as a result of their marriages, gained two new friends. I have two of the loveliest sisters-in-law in the whole world. These friendships have had over 20 years to grow. My first sister-in-law taught, and continues to teach, me how to be inviting.

I had the privilege of meeting my first sister when I was 14. I had grown up with two brothers and had never had a sister. Fourteen is an awkward age. I was definitely an awkward teenager. I was tall and gangly and more interested in books and school than social status. I had great friends but many things were beginning to change around me. Iris was always so glad to see me. She always had a kind word for me and was just so sweet. The day that she and my brother got married was one of the happiest days of my life. Now she truly was my sister and an official part of my family.

As the years went by we enjoyed each other's company. She and my brother were young when they married, and also very fun. I had gone off to college but whenever I came home they were there to greet me and welcome me into their home. In my mind they had a perfect marriage, a small apartment, and a life that had many possibilities. I longed for each of these things. We had no idea that my life path would be drastically different. Iris brought the first grandchild, my niece, into the family. We all shared such excitement over that first bundle of joy!

Iris was transparent in her life, her marriage, her parenting. No topic was off limits and she was always so glad to see me. We would enjoy cups of tea together and smile over the antics of the family. As much as my mother was determined and strong-willed, Iris was accommodating and yielding.

In my 20s my brother and Iris moved to the Pacific Northwest to be near her family. We were sad to see them go, but now the visits were much more intentional and fun. Two more girls were born and I loved being an aunt and seeing how much these little people were just like me even though

I had not birthed them. (I kept waiting to meet Mr. Right but only Mr. Wrongs kept showing up.) Months would go be when Iris and I would not talk because of busy schedules and time zone differences. As I was living my single life, traveling all over the country, taking different jobs and opportunities, one of my choices landed me in their very small town living with my brother and his family.

Sometimes a haven is provided for you when you do not even know you need one. I had been working in high-pressured schools and dealing with very busy cities, and their little island town was such a contrast. There was no Wal-Mart to race off to if I needed something. Everything had to slow down and I realized I did not know how to do that. Iris was such a help. I worked only three days a week and, as I lived with my brother and sister-in-law, I was home with her four days a week. That year was and has continued to be one of the most fun years of my life.

We absolutely did life together. Just as any household does, we had our ups and our downs. But Iris welcomed me in without batting an eye. I helped where I could and I stayed out when I could. I know not every relationship can withstand living in such close quarters, but for us that year it was the right thing.

Every day I would think about how I wanted to be this inviting to someone who needed a place to live. I would want my guests to feel special on their birthdays, I would want them to lounge around on a Sunday morning with the family, and I would want them to feel like they could cook in my kitchen. Iris offered such things to me month after month after month. We both grew so much as women that year. We were constantly reminded of the benefits of the other's life and then the benefits of our own.

There are many stories of how Iris has touched my life. Just a few years ago, we had the terrible experience of losing my mother to cancer. It was discovered in April and by July the whole family was coming together to give their last respects. Iris, my brother, and their three daughters drove from the Pacific Northwest and stayed with me at my house.

The weather was over 100 degrees, my air conditioning went out on the day they arrived, two days after that my house was literally overrun by ants, the living room flooded with water and soot from the makeshift air conditioner in the fireplace, and the washing machine stopped working. All of this happened on top of the anguish of losing our mother.

As if this were not enough, Iris was struggling with some serious gall bladder issues. The only clue I had that Iris was not 100% well was that she wore yoga pants instead of her usual cute attire. I felt terrible that my house was falling apart while I had guests. Iris handled each issue in stride. She suggested we take everyone to Target to get out of the heat, and she helped me haul laundry over to a friend's house, as everything needed to be washed because of the ants. And then she helped me mop up my tile floors so that soot would not get tracked into every room of the house. Whenever I would thank her for helping she would respond with, "Of course, this is what we do for each other, we support each other."

This is what we do, we support each other. Just recently I got married and Iris threw a bridal shower for me. As the hostess she had each person share something about me as I opened their gift. When I got to her gift she shared that it has been a long journey the two of us. I had the privilege of living in the incubator with her as she discovered the highs and lows of marriage, raising kids, and losing parents. "I am so glad you are my sister-in-law, and please learn from my mistakes since you got to see them up close and personal." This made me smile because I was thinking that I had learned so much from her. Not her mistakes, but all the things she had done right.

Her spirit of hospitality and desire to keep everyone happy are two of her greater strengths. Often I will stop to think about how Iris would approach a neighbor or a friend, when someone in my world is struggling. Because of our many years of friendship, I have many instances to pull up and to contemplate. I want to be known as someone who is inviting. I still struggle with this but thankfully Iris will be in my life for many more years as well.

Chapter 5

Adventuresome Addie

Adventures are unique and fun. The people, the event, the timing of life all play into the level of adventure that we can experience. We create or squelch our opportunities for adventure. In the movie *The Holiday* there is a scene when one of the main characters, Iris, is getting some advice from an elderly gentleman named Arthur over dinner. Iris has become upset as she tells him about her old boyfriend who got engaged and did not tell her. This exchange follows:

Arthur: He's a schmuck.

Iris: As a matter of fact, he is a huge schmuck, how did you know?

Arthur: He let you go, this is not a hard one to figure out. Iris, in the movies we have leading ladies and we have the best friend. You, I can tell, are a

> leading lady, but for some reason you are behaving like the best friend.
>
> Iris: You are so right. You're supposed to be the leading lady of your own life!"[3]

That is Addie. She is the leading lady of her own life, without any apologies. If any event needs to be more fun then invite Addie into the mix and adventure will be sure to follow.

We are all so different from one another. Sometimes it is difficult to find common ground when someone is very different. When I was younger I wanted my friends to be similar to me, but over the years I have learned it is much more exciting if a friend is vastly different.

I often will admire a trait in another woman and not believe that I am capable of cultivating that trait. Adventuresome Addie taught me otherwise. She is my other lovely sister-in-law. She is thoughtful, funny, and loves to have a good time. The crazier the adventure the better the time, in her opinion. We have always been drastically different, but I have learned much from her and the way that she approaches life.

Adventuresome Addie is one of the most amazing people I know. She lives life constantly thinking, "How can I break that rule?" I have always been a law abider. I am told that when I was a very small child I only had to be looked at sternly to be disciplined. If I were told I should not do something, I agreed and walked away. Even now if an open door is marked

---

[3] Nancy Meyers, Director. 2006. *The Holiday* [Motion Picture]. USA: Universal Pictures.

Exit Only, I will not enter. I will walk all the way around the building to enter at the designated point.

As I have grown older I have realized that I carry a fear about doing the wrong thing. I do not ever want to do the wrong thing, and I worry that I will. One day I was expressing this to Addie. As I was explaining about how I constantly worry about doing the wrong thing, this huge grin formed on her face. "Why are you smiling so much?" I asked her.

She shook her head and said, "I cannot believe you walk around worrying about that all the time. You always do the right thing. I worry for you because you never do the wrong thing!" As you can imagine we dived into a very deep, probing conversation trying to understand the other person's perspective.

It was during this conversation that Addie explained she immediately thinks about how she can break a rule as soon as she hears it. Addie was key in helping me find enough freedom in myself to unreservedly date and possibly, maybe, meet the right person.

I had been raised in a very conservative way. The woman is the helpmate to the man and that is her role in life. I was not one to question the system. My mom had married at 21 and raised a family with my dad. I would do the same. Except I was not dating anyone at 18 or 19, or 21, or 25, or 35. My dream was not coming true. I went to college, I earned a degree, I was developing my career but literally with each step I was thinking, "I will do this until I meet Mr. Right and then I will do married life." I will not get into all the reasons why that thinking was so detrimental, but believe me, it was.

I had been raised with the idea that God would bring me the right man. But I did not realize that because of my fear of dating the wrong one or choosing the wrong one I had built walls up all around myself. Addie and I were on a very long road trip. We had hours and hours to talk. We had been in each other's life for over 20 years since she had married my brother. Sometimes a friendship grows slower and deeper than you can even imagine.

It was during this road trip that we discovered how differently we looked at life. I was constantly asking, "How can I abide by all the rules?" and she was constantly thinking, "How can I break all the rules?" It was so enlightening to stop and try to see the world through a different pair of glasses. I did not even know this rebellious pair of glasses existed. The more we talked, the more we began to understand each other. We brought up specific instances where our lives had intersected and we had totally misunderstood the other's intent. We swapped places. We talked about hundreds of different circumstances and traded glasses. I really purposed to look at the situation from the perspective of trying to break the rules, and she tried to look at it from the perspective of not questioning the rules.

Relief flooded the car. We finally had a basis for understanding each other. Now we really began to dig into topics. I brought up my situation in dating. Addie really wanted me to have lots of dates. She challenged me to take on her perspective. If I were to break all the rules I had known about dating up to this point, what would my dating life look like? This was an interesting thought. She also challenged me to look outside my faith. But . . . but . . . but . . . ! All of these excuses wanted to spill out of me as to why I could not do that. But in the end she was right. I needed a different perspective. My position was that I would know on the first date if I would want to marry him or not, and she pointed out that is way too much pressure for a first date.

After our trip I returned home and signed up with a dating service. The goal was dates. Many of them. Addie had challenged me to have 10 dates in one week. I began. My whole thinking had changed. I no longer was looking for Mr. Right. I was looking for one first date over and over and over. It was through this process that I met the man who would become my husband. By changing my perspective, my walls fell away and I was able to relax and just be me. Because I was trying to break the rules I actually relaxed more and was not so tense as when trying to follow the rules.

What is so interesting to me is that my husband is all the things I worried I would not find in a man. He is strong in faith, he loves me, and he absolutely balances my personality. At times he is more of a rule follower than I am but it works for us.

Now as I live my life I have two lenses of perspective to look through. My natural one is the follow-the-rules lens. But the second perspective is the rules-are-meant-to-be-broken lens. I have to admit, sometimes that lens is a lot more fun.

Addie has brought a depth and richness to my life. We mature as people yet sometimes we hang onto childish or wrongly-perceived truths about the world. I had done this. In so many ways I was still viewing the world as I had when I was 17. The world has changed, I have changed. Addie helped me recalibrate my thinking, not to match hers, but to a perspective of my own. If someone had asked me if I thought for myself, I would have said yes. But looking back, I was thinking the way everyone expected me to think, or the way I perceived everyone wanted me to think. Discovering a different perspective and having it modeled in front of me for so many years has allowed me to look at topics and issues from several angles and then make an opinion.

What would a friendship be that would feel so drastic or so different for you? Can you even define it or describe it? I would not have been able to, but that is the beauty of pursuing the friendships that are right in front of you. Who is standing in front of you in your world? Is there someone in your family or neighborhood that just seems different than you? I would encourage you to become friends with her. Learn from her perspective and grow as a woman.

Chapter 6

Mirror Mira

Mirrors have many uses in our lives. Mirrors reflect who we are. They can show us our blemishes or our beauty depending on where the looker chooses to focus. When a mirror is clear and clean the reflected image is almost identical to the original. When the mirror is distorted and blurry it is difficult to get a sense of what the original looks like. Several weeks ago my husband and I were at the zoo. In one particular corner there was a small resource center. There was a set of distorted mirrors. I am quite tall, but as I walked past these mirrors my shape went from tall and sweeping to short and squatty. The one that made me laugh the most was the last. The way the mirror was distorted it made me look like an hour glass, a very elongated hourglass. What's my point? My point is that the quality of the mirror matters. When I am getting ready for an important event I want a mirror that will show me the truest reflection of myself I can find. Mira is often my true reflection.

As different as Addie and I are, Mira and I are incredibly similar, almost identical at times. Mirror Mira is often the mirror into my soul. Our lives run on these parallel tracks that are so similar and yet so different.

Mira is about ten years older than I am. She has often helped me steer clear of a bad decision because she is far enough ahead to see the long term consequences of a choice. Over the years I have learned to deeply love and appreciate her listening ear, her words of wisdom, and her amazing sense of humor.

Mira and I became aware of each other when I was a college student and she was an assisting professor. About ten years went by and then our paths crossed again. I was working a job that was incredibly stressful, but the local college offered a mentoring program for new hires like me. Mira approached me about being my mentor through this job and I accepted. We had regular meetings to discuss the pressing issues of my job. I would explain my struggles and she would offer ideas and suggestions of how to overcome and solve the issues.

Meeting on a regular basis is an excellent way to build new friendships. What was so interesting about this friendship is that neither one of us realized we were building one. We thought we were building a working relationship. For nine months we met on a biweekly basis. As things turned out, I ended up resigning from that job and losing Mira as my mentor. On our last meeting, I wanted to express how much she had helped me and taught me. To my great surprise and shock she expressed the same thing. At first I couldn't even comprehend what she was saying, she had learned from me? But it was true, I had learned from her and she had learned from me. Her experiences had taught me how to deal with new problems and my ability to deal with the problems had taught her to continue to grow.

We both agreed that we needed to continue to be friends and meet on a regular basis. Our lives were so different. She had been married for years. I was single. She was the mother of three almost-grown children and had a huge family. I lived alone and had only my parents and grandparents close by.

She had a thriving career and was very well known in the community. I had just resigned from my job and did not know where I was heading next. Despite these enormous differences, we had commonality.

We both loved people, we loved the world of early childhood development. We often had too much to say. We wanted to please God with our actions. We wanted to love our families as best we could and be content in our lives.

If you are struggling to be content in your life, find another woman whose life is very different from yours. And then meet on a regular basis. Just talk about your lives. It will help you to realize that your life may have some challenges and difficulties but it is manageable. When you hear about someone else's life and struggles, you realize there are pros and cons to each and every situation. By having this contrasting friend you also can learn to appreciate the differences. So often the things I longed for were the very things Mira wanted to trade out of her life.

An example of this was that I lived alone and Mira had 12 different people under her roof. Most of them were family but a few were people needing a place to stay on their journey through life. Her family had a single friend who had suffered severe hearing loss he lived across town. They often would invite him places and take him on outings. Mira would get so frustrated whenever they took him back to his home. He always wanted them to come in, or do one more thing before returning home. Mira just could not understand it. The kids were fighting in the back seat, she was exhausted, they had already done all sorts of fun things. Nothing exciting was happening when they got home, everyone was just going to bed. Often Mira admitted that she was silently fuming, "GO HOME! And be grateful we invited you to come along at all!" We can be so lovely when we are exhausted. Thankfully she had enough wisdom to keep her thoughts to herself.

One day over coffee she was sharing her frustrations about this situation with me. I smiled at her and said, "I get it."

She stared at me and said, "Then please explain it to me because I want to understand it, too!" I retraced her steps. I explained that it was generous of them to invite him and that he did appreciate it. But at the end of the night he was facing a cold, dark, quiet house. There would be no one wanting to hear about his adventure or the fun he had. The contrast was too great and his emotions were getting the better of him. Mira's response was so memorable to me. She said, "But the kids are fighting in the back seat, he wants that?"

I replied with, "Of course he does. He wishes he had a family to shush and to take home to put to bed."

We continued to talk back and forth for several minutes. Finally Mira asked, "How do you understand this so well?"

I said, "Because I experience it every time someone drops me off from having a good time. I work very hard at controlling my emotions until I get into the house, because I am grateful

I was invited. I'm grateful they thought of me, but I still have to walk into the darkness and face the loneliness."

Mira shook her head back and forth and said, "I'm sorry. I had no idea. Thank you for explaining this to me."

Several months later she told me that they had changed the way they take their friend home after an event. Instead of dropping him off while everyone is in the car, they actually take him to their house. They let him watch the putting to bed of kids, and the nightly brushing of the teeth. They let him witness the shutting down of everyone's lives. Then two of them take him home, pull into the driveway, walk him inside, turn on a few lights, and visit for about five minutes. Then they say good-bye to him, give him a hug and let him walk them to the door. She could not believe the difference that it has made in the whole evening and his demeanor. Mira said, "I never would have understood this without you being so transparent. Thank you."

Another very interesting example of unique similarities is Mira's education and mine. She had never earned a bachelor's degree but because she was so well known in the community she had been promoted to positions that normally required a four-year degree. She was beginning to get pressure from her superiors to complete her education and earn a bachelor's degree.

I had earned a four-year degree but was wanting to make a career change. For logistical reasons I had to get a second bachelor's degree before I could move on to get a master's degree. It was during one of our coffee runs that Mira and I realized we both needed to head back to school within the next year.

We talked through the pros and cons and what each of us needed. We both needed 60 units. Neither of us wanted to start back at the beginning. I agreed to do the research of finding some options, she agreed to be the transportation and give honest feedback. Within just a few weeks I found an adult learning program that was accelerated. Classes met once a week for three to four hours. A typical program took about 16 months to complete. We went to the orientation meeting and were ready to sign up.

But Mirror Mira and I were about to look into the mirror, we just did not know it yet. The meeting we had chosen to go to was a Bachelor of Arts in Education. As the meeting progressed and questions were answered I began to think, "This is not what I want to do. I have been teaching for 10 years. I want to do something else." But Mira and I had agreed to do it together. I sat through the rest of the meeting twisted up in knots. This was not the program I wanted.

The presenter explained that there was a second degree that they were just beginning to offer that was in Organizational Systems. If we wanted to stay for that meeting as well, we were welcome. During the ten-minute intermission between meetings I turned to Mira and said, "I am not interested in this first degree."

Mira looked right into my eyes and said, "Neither am I."

Wait, what?! Blinking I said, "You mean this isn't the degree you want to pursue?"

Mira shook her head. She suggested we stay for the second meeting and see what we thought.

By the end of the second meeting we were both convinced this was the meeting we were supposed to attend. I was confident this was the program I wanted, would Mira mirror my confidence for herself? Absolutely. We both filled out our paperwork and put the wheels in motion to return to school. We met on a weekly basis now: Mira would pick me up, we would grab a bite to eat, and then we would head to class.

We thought we had a close friendship before this experience but attending school together cemented it for us. There is something about working towards a specific goal with a very dear friend for an extended period of time that cannot be described. There were times when I did not think I was going to make it, and there were times when Mira did not think she was going to make it. But make it we did. Earning that bachelor's degree has changed both of our lives. We are both so grateful to the other for walking through that experience together. Having a friend who mirrors your goals and desires is a rich blessing indeed.

What is also interesting about Mira and me is that we mirror negative emotions as well. So often over the past 15 years I would call to gripe about something and she would be silent on the other end. I would wonder why, but then she would explain that she had been struggling with the very same emotions. But because our lives are so different, we could more clearly see into the other person's situation. Often she would have excellent words of wisdom for me, and vice versa.

If you are an emotional woman, it is important for you to have a friend who can relate to your emotions. Mira and I joke that we are each other's barometers. We call each other to get honest feedback about our emotions. There have been times that I have observed that Mira's emotions are a bit overreactive and the situation is not as dire as it feels. She can hear this from me because I have the same emotions. But there have been other situations when I have encouraged her to be a bit more incensed by what has happened. Validation can be a very valuable thing. Start looking around for a friend that is similar to your disposition. If she is a woman of wisdom, I would encourage you to plan an invasion and invite her to get a cup of coffee with you.

Chapter 7

Precisely Private Vivian

I have always been a person who wears her heart on her sleeve. Poker is a terrible game for me because my face gives away my hand before the first card hits the table. I also struggle with the obligation to answer any question asked of me, whether deeply personal or otherwise. If I have the answer I should comply. I have lived so much of my life compelled by these obligations to other people, it had never even occurred to me that privacy, or the depth of privacy I want in my life, is a choice.

Precisely Private Vivian taught me the value and technique of not answering every question asked of me. She taught me through example, conversation, and some reproof. We were roommates, and as roommates we knew way more about each other's lives than the greater population. Just in the happenstance of living, we observed interaction with family members. A roommate hangs up the phone from an upsetting phone call, and the other is standing there wanting to offer help, kindness, or silence.

We had a friendship such as this. Our lives were very different, but we shared many of the same interests. We enjoyed single life and the freedom it offered us. Our social circles were different but we encountered many of the same people in daily living.

We viewed the world differently, and we approached it and walked through it even more differently. Sometimes the differences were the greatest strength of our friendship and sometimes they were our greatest weakness or wedge.

Because I am a pleaser, I would answer any question from any person at any time. Vivian was much different. She decided what information people would have and when. She saw her world as exactly *her* world. She would decide whom she would and would not invite into it. I, on the other hand, could barely comprehend this. How was this even possible? I was about to learn.

Vivian was very well known in the community and there were seasons of the year that she was often in the spotlight. She did not enjoy the spotlight and gladly would have lived her life without its glare. But there were times it could not be avoided. She and I began to notice a pattern develop.

- Vivian would be in the spotlight, maybe because of a newspaper article or an interview.
- People would want to know more.
- Vivian would not answer their questions or engage them any further.
- People realized we were roommates.
- I would get pumped for information.

- I would supply information, not realizing Vivian had chosen to withhold it.
- People would return to Vivian and blurt out whatever information they had weaseled out of me.
- Vivian and I would have conflict at home.

I hate conflict. I would rather hash it out, get it over with, ask for forgiveness, become friends again, and then move on in life. It is also important to me to learn from mistakes and not make them over and over again.

The cycle repeated several times before Vivian and I were able to pinpoint the problem and find a solution. Through several discussions we were able to recognize the extreme difference between our behavior in a conversation. She could not understand why I would so willing give information up, and I could not understand how she was able to keep it so private. The wonderful thing about a true friendship is that Vivian knew that I had no ill will towards her. Especially after we talked, she realized I did not even know that I was offending her when I answered questions. I actually thought I was helping her! The irony of life sometimes.

Now we both understood the other's motives and intent. But we still had an impasse. I did not have the finesse to gracefully get out of people's questions. I felt like I would be rude to just walk away. Together, Vivian and I made a plan.

An interview was coming up and we must break the cycle. Because I was the one divulging too much information, I knew it was up to me. At home, Vivian and I practiced. She would ask me questions and I would practice changing the subject or finding an excuse to get out of the conversation. I felt prepared and ready.

Spotlight shone on Vivian. She deflected questions. People sought me out. Information was requested. I deflected a round of questions. More intense questions flew at me. I faltered a bit but held my ground. People were ravenous, they wanted information and they were going to squeeze it out of me. I refused. I finally excused myself, went to my car and cried. What had just happened? We had a plan, what had gone wrong? I replayed the incident in my mind. I had not given up any information but I felt like a wreck inside.

I drove home, preparing myself for the worst. Disappointing people is so hard for me, I just hate it. Vivian was already home. Immediately she could tell I was not okay. I spilled out the whole story to her. Every last detail was described. I was just a heap sitting at the kitchen table, waiting for my judgment sentence.

True friendship is such a beautiful thing. Precisely Private Vivian reached across the table, took my hands, looked me in the eye and said, "I am so proud of you. Thank you for protecting my privacy for me." I was shocked! Wait, what just happened?

I blinked my eyes to clear my head and asked, "You are okay with how this happened?" Vivian nodded her head. Relief washed over me.

We continued to talk about what had happened and through Vivian's insightfulness we realized I was so upset because I felt I had been rude and I felt a bit badgered. Vivian had told me several weeks earlier that information is power and some people will do whatever they have to get information.

What I had experienced was the intensity of this attempt to acquire information. We changed the plan.

Vivian and I worked together to come up with one sentence to respond to any question, at any time, in any situation. If someone asked me about her life the standard answer became, "I'm sorry I cannot answer that question, you will have to talk to Vivian about that." Done. This short, precise response helped me immensely. It filled my need to be gracious to people, but it did not crack the door open for me to spill any information accidentally.

Another big opportunity was quickly approaching. Again Vivian helped me practice at home by asking all kinds of questions, and I answered very consistently, "I'm sorry I cannot answer that question, you will have to talk to Vivian about that." I was ready.

An article in the newspaper came out and Vivian was the topic of many conversations. Humans are so predictable. If something has worked once than surely it will work again. But today was not that day. At the supermarket I ran into a friend Vivian and I had in common. The questions began, "She seems like such a lovely woman, is she going to keep working at the job she currently has?"

I smiled and said, "I'm sorry I cannot answer that question, you will have to talk to Vivian about that."

The woman smiled. "Is Vivian dating anyone?"

"I'm sorry I cannot answer that question, you will have to talk to Vivian about that."

The woman continued, "Her parents have not been at church lately, do you know why?"

My reply (yes, you guessed it): "I'm sorry I cannot answer that question, you will have to talk to Vivian about that."

This went on for several minutes the other woman kept asking questions, I kept replying with the same response. "How long do you think you'll be living with Vivian?" asked the woman, but then she raised her hand up in a stop gesture and said, "Wait let me guess, I will have to talk to Vivian about that."

I smiled and said, "Yes, that's correct." Slowly turning my grocery cart in the opposite direction I offered over my shoulder, "It was nice talking with you, I hope you have a nice day." And left.

Word got around quickly that I was no longer the person to go for information. This greatly pleased both Vivian and me.

Many years later Precisely Private Vivian got to see her coaching in action. Both of my parents had passed away suddenly. It was a shock to our family and our community. One Sunday at church I was reconnecting with Vivian. It had been several months since we had seen each other. An acquaintance to our family whom I had not seen in over 20 years came over to offer her condolences.

As Vivian and I were in conversation, the acquaintance approached.

Acquaintance: "Oh honey, I am so sorry for your loss."

I turned towards the woman and replied: "Thank you, I appreciate that."

Acquaintance: "What are you going to do with yourself now that you are all alone?"

My reply: "I will figure it out."

Acquaintance: "Your brother lives in Seattle, are you going to go live with him?"

My reply: "I will figure it out."

Acquaintance: "What are you doing right now? Are you working? Are you dating anyone?"

My reply: "I believe you came over to offer your condolences. You've done that. I appreciate that you missed my parents. If you'll excuse me, I was in the middle of a conversation when you walked up and I would like to finish that conversation."

Acquaintance: "Oh, forgive me, of course. Take care, honey." And the acquaintance quickly left.

I turned back to finish my conversation with Vivian. Her mouth was wide open. She stammered out, "I cannot believe you just did that! I'm so proud of you. You were absolutely right in everything you said."

A few tears trickled out for various and assorted reasons, but I smiled. Winking, I said, "You taught me everything I know," which in that situation at that moment was absolutely true. As Vivian and I embraced, I thought about how friendships are precious and their gifts are invaluable. And you just never know when you are going to need that special something learned from a friend to get through that next difficult whatever.

CHAPTER 8

Prayer Warrior Wendy

"Prayer changes things; I don't know how, but it does." Every Wednesday evening Pastor John Mincy would say this. It is true. Pray does change things. So often I want prayer to be my wishlist, telling God all the things I want for Christmas. But prayer is fellowship with God. Prayer is our way of communicating with the one who created us. I am like any woman. I have seasons where I pray very diligently in a very specific way. But then I have other seasons when it seems that all I manage to do consistently is fling my dire needs up to God. Having a friend to pray with and talk with really helps put the sacredness of prayer into perspective.

I would really struggle to be friends with someone who only called every time she was in trouble. I would also struggle to be friends with someone who only talked about herself every time we got together. Thankfully, God is more faithful and patient than I am, and prayer changes things.

Prayer is a spiritual discipline that I know I should practice. I think we all go through seasons of being consistent and being inconsistent with prayer. I struggle to control my thoughts, as many women do. I have learned over the years that if I have another woman to pray with regularly, it helps on both fronts. I become more consistent in prayer because I deeply care about this woman, and I pray for her when I cannot control my own thoughts. So often I bring wisdom into her life and she brings wisdom into mine because we are consistently praying for each other.

Wendy the Warrior was one of the most lovely friends I have ever had. I want to share how we became friends. I was 31 and single. I was trapped in a bad friendship/relationship with a man that I just could not seem to get free of. Over the years I had noticed that women who were married to police officers or firemen had a different level of marriage than other couples. I realized that this was because the couple knew that one of them could die on the job. Thus they kept a short account of wrongs, and really worked to know each other and love each other on a daily basis.

I wanted that kind of relationship. I hoped to get married in the future and I knew I had some things to learn. I began my search. Who had this type of strong marital relationship? Several weeks went by and then suddenly I knew.

I worked at a school and I had had several students from the same family. They were always around. I would see them at football games, church, and school outings. As a whole, they seemed pretty happy. One night at a volleyball game I gathered my courage. I sat down next to Wendy and asked, "I have a strange request. I would like you to think about it and then give me an answer in a few days." Wendy smiled and nodded her head receptively. I continued, "I have observed that you and your husband have an excellent relationship. I would like to learn how you do it. I was wondering if we could meet once a week for coffee and just talk. That's my request, please think about it."

There was utter bewilderment on Wendy's face. She said, "I was just asked to be a Bible Study Fellowship leader today, and now you're asking me this. I'm quite overwhelmed. I'll need some time to think about. If I had to give you an answer right now I would say no, but if I can have some time to think about it, that would be great." I agreed, thanked her for listening to my request, and then got up and left.

This was a first for me. I had never gotten this kind of response before, I had always gotten a yes. But I reminded myself that she had not said no, she had just said she needed some time.

Several weeks went by, I think it was about five. I was beginning to think she had forgotten, but she had not. One afternoon right before Christmas, she and her daughter came into my classroom. I was having a very emotional day. My first thought was, "Oh no, not today, if she tells me she can't do it, I'll cry and be so embarrassed." We sat down together.

Wendy began very slowly. "I have thought about your request so much. That was such an overwhelming day for me, first with the leadership request and then with your unique request. As I have prayed about it all and thought about it all I have decided that I would like to meet with you once a week." Relief flooded over me. Wendy continued, "I'm very busy so it would be best for me if we could pick a specific time and meet the same time each week." That was perfect, I was so excited. I opened my mouth to tell her how glad I was, and tears started flowing out of my eyes instead. Wendy immediately grabbed some tissues for me and said, "Curl your toes. I know it sounds silly, but somehow curling your toes helps the tears to stop." So I did. I curled my toes and blinked and sniffed and wiped my eyes. I was so incredibly embarrassed.

I was finally able to stammer out, "Thank you, as you can see this means a lot to me. I have been emotional all day," (deep breath) "but thank you." We smiled at each other. We looked at our schedules and decided that Thursday mornings at eight o'clock we would meet. We would meet for 45 minutes because I had to teach a class at 8:50. For the next three years we rarely missed a Thursday morning. People would try to schedule a meeting or activity and I would say, "I'm sorry, I'm not available." That was all. I even told my boss this when he asked to schedule a meeting. Later he congratulated me on keeping true to what was important to me.

The Thursday morning began with me spilling over with many, many words. On the very first meeting, Wendy asked for one thing that she could pray about for me throughout the week. As I sifted through all the things that had landed on the table between us, I thoughtfully chose one. Wendy wrote it down on a post it note and promised that she would pray for me throughout the week. The bell rang and our first meeting was over. As Wendy was leaving I realized I had not asked her what she needed prayer about. I purposed the following week to ask that question right at the beginning.

This is how our friendship evolved. Each week we would swap prayer requests based on what we had shared in the last 40 minutes. I had thought we would pray together, as this is what I had often done in the past with friends, but Wendy did not feel comfortable with praying out loud, and she promised to pray diligently for me throughout the week.

What did I learn from Wendy the Warrior? I learned that friendship is sweet and slow. She was a very slow processor and I was a very fast processor. We learned to strengthen our traits, I slowing to think about things and Wendy trusting her instincts to make a quicker decision now and then. I learned that there is a sweetness to having a friend whom you can trust utterly and who does not judge you. Because of my tears at our very first "chat" it gave our friendship a level of vulnerability that is hard to reach sometimes.

Safe. I felt safe. I felt safe to tell her my dreams. I felt safe to tell her my fears. I felt safe to share the deepest parts of my soul. As we met weekly and shared our most pressing prayer request, we discovered safety in speaking the truth to each other; and we discovered the safety of trusting God with our most heartfelt requests. My favorite thing was when we had been praying about something and one of us would call the other and say, "Guess what? God did it! He absolutely answered our prayers." And the other would always respond with, "Tell me all about it, don't leave out one detail."

I moved away but we still talk on the phone occasionally. I think of her every Thursday and I miss her. God did bless me with a husband, and I often think back to my conversations with Wendy. She taught me so much by just being my friend, and being willing to say yes to an odd request. I sought her out with the idea of learning from her marriage, and Wendy was very gracious and open in sharing wisdom from her relationship. But I got even more than I bargained for, in a friendship that demonstrated the power of prayer. This has proven to be the greater blessing of the two, having a friend who diligently and faithfully prays.

I had pursued a friendship with Wendy because I felt that she was a wise woman and I could learn from her. Mentoring is such a two-way street. Just this past fall Wendy needed my wisdom, experience, and prayers. Her parents had just celebrated their 50th wedding anniversary and then her father suddenly passed away. It shocked everyone. Wendy called me and said, "I wanted to call you because you know exactly how this feels and I need to know you are praying for me." I assured her I was praying and would continue to do so. Wendy had been a pillar of strength for me after my parents had passed away and now I had the opportunity to be the same for her.

Having these in-depth friendships brings an uncharacteristic value to situations. Loss is so painful when it is happening to you, yet to be prepared to help and support a friend when she suffers the same loss is invaluable. Do you have a friend or friends like this? When life crumbles in around you, whom do you call? Who is your support? If no names or faces come to mind, I strongly encourage you to begin looking around you. Potential deep friendships are all around us, we just have to look and be willing to pursue them.

CHAPTER 9

GRIEF AND GRATITUDE GRETCHEN

Some emotions are harder than others to understand and deal with. Having a loving friend to walk with through the tough valleys and then the incredible heights of life is an amazing thing.

As I experience my journey through life, grief and gratitude often travel as unlikely companions in the same vehicle. If you have suffered grief, I hope you will know what I am talking about. Grief is a necessary emotion or group of emotions that each of us has to work through when a loss occurs. Grief requires us to land at the bottom of the barrel, to wallow in the sadness. For some the wallowing is only a few days but for others it is months or even years. In my own personal experience gratitude is the ladder out of the barrel. Gratitude leads me back to normal life and the surprising beauty the loss created. But gratitude has to be consciously sought after while grief, on the other hand, just slides right in at the most unexpected times. Cultivating a life of gratitude is something I have always wanted. It is an ongoing process, but a process definitely worth pursuing and refining and developing.

Grief and Gratitude Gretchen has modeled these two traits for me very well. Our story began when she was friends with one of my roommates. She would come over to hang out with my roommate and I usually stuck around to enjoy the fun. Our paths loosely crossed for about a year. One beautiful May day a call came in for Gretchen. I happened to be working in the same building where Gretchen taught school. I went and found her, and stood in her classroom while she took the phone call. That phone call changed her life forever.

Unexpectedly that morning Gretchen's father had died. He said his chest hurt, he sat down in a chair, and minutes later he was dead. Everything shifted for Gretchen at that moment. I was working as a substitute teacher. I was assigned to her class and she was out for the next two weeks.

I knew Gretchen, but not very well, and I couldn't imagine losing my dad so suddenly. I did know Gretchen liked lip gloss, so one day at the market I bought her four different flavors. She would come into her classroom every few days to check on the students' coursework and we would chat. Each day I saw her, I would give her a lip gloss. It made her smile each time and she would say, "I hadn't smiled yet today, thanks." A few weeks later I found some chocolate shaped like first-aid bandages, called "Boo-boo Bandages" I wrote a little note explaining they were for her heart, and what better thing for a woman's heart than chocolate.

With each of these gifts I had no idea what I was doing, I just knew I had to do something. I couldn't sit by and let my friend feel sad and hurt without doing something. This was a very important thing to learn. When someone is hurting, especially a friend in the sisterhood, do something. I had also purposed to be around after all the condolences ran out. It is common for everyone to rally around at the beginning of the grief cycle, but then people get busy and refocus on their lives and forget that their friend is still grappling with the fact that her life will never be the same.

Several weeks after the memorial service I called Gretchen to see if she would like to go out for coffee. She accepted and a wonderful friendship began to bloom and blossom. We soon discovered that we could laugh together. Oh my goodness, could we laugh. We loved to share stories about our lives and then rollick in the utter mayhem and ridiculousness of those adventures. She was an avid reader like me, and so we began swapping books. We would meet up at church and sit together. And we loved food, too much at times.

She made it through the first year of grief. The first year is the hardest, so the experts and everyone else always say. Gretchen had followed the grief rule of not making any major changes in her life. But as that first year of grief came to a close she had some huge changes in mind for herself. She had been a literature teacher for several years. But she knew it wasn't what she wanted to do for the rest of her life. She applied to beauty school and within nine months had completed the course and began a practicum in the local salon. Her family flipped out. Why was she doing this? She was throwing her career away. She should be more responsible.

Gretchen had this iron determination. I could see it on her face; I could hear it in her voice. She was going to do it. One evening when we were sharing dinner, we were discussing this huge life change. I asked her why she did it, what was the motivation?

Her response was this: "My dad changed so many people's lives by being a pastor and caring for them. I have that same desire. I want to care for people. When I was a teacher I was educating people but I wasn't caring for them the way I wanted to. I want to help people feel better about themselves and see the beauty they already have." I loved this answer. I had so much admiration for Gretchen. She was younger than I was and yet she was making huge life-changing decisions, and succeeding.

During the year that she was completing her cosmetology license another tragedy struck our lives. One of our really close friends was diagnosed with breast cancer. She was 33 years old, vibrant, beautiful, and one of the most inspiring people you could ever meet. She fought for two years, suffered through two rounds of chemo and two rounds of radiation, and lost her battle. That friendship between the three of us was one of the most beautiful things I've been part of. Gretchen discovered during this time that she absolutely, positively was on the right track. She would visit our friend who was suffering and give her facials and pedicures. She would help groom her wigs, she would make our suffering, deflated friend feel beautiful. One of my favorite things that year was to go over to my friend's house, lie on the bed with her because she was so tired, and listen to her tell me about Gretchen's visits. For just a few short minutes every now and then my friend would forget that she had cancer and enjoy the feminine pleasures of being a woman.

This is friendship. This is what we are called to do, to nurture and to bless those around us. One evening a few months after the second round of treatment, I received a call from Gretchen. Our friend was in the hospital and the end was near. Gretchen's life had changed so much by now. She had moved to the city, had found an apprenticeship in a fancy, well-to-do salon and was making her dream come true. It was such an interesting season in our friendship as together we watched one of our friends die, Gretchen being so familiar with grief, and me, hardly at all.

Grief and Gratitude. It is interesting that these two characteristics often go hand in hand. My life had changed quite a bit as well. I had welcomed two little boys into my home and was hoping to adopt them. The week that my friend passed away, I also found out that the boys would be returning to their biological parents. I was devastated. No one knew the time frame of the boys' departure, but it was inevitable. My journey of grief was beginning. Gretchen would be the one who consistently brought gratitude back into my world.

Four months later, my boys were gone. I was alone again. I thought the grief was going to swallow me up whole. Gretchen was now living in a beach city of Southern California and she suggested I come for a visit. So I did. We went to Disneyland, we ate great food, and we painted on the beach. It was a very memorable weekend. Sometimes we would talk, sometimes we wouldn't. We had done enough of life together to know what was appropriate, and when. Even though no one else had died in my life, I felt like it. I had always dreamed of being a mother and now that dream was gone.

I followed the rules of the cycles of grief. I returned to my classroom, I made no sudden changes, even though I would cry every day as I drove to school because my little boys were no longer with me. I missed the giggling and fighting in the backseat. I plowed through. Even though Gretchen lived several hours away, she consistently came to see me. We would do the things we loved to do, we would eat, watch movies, and talk about books. And our friendship grew as I headed into the hardest season of my life. I don't think either one of us was prepared for what was coming.

In the tenth month of my year of grief, my mom headed into the hospital for a routine hysterectomy. There was nothing routine about it. On April 9, 2010 a whole new wave of grief flooded into my world. My mom had cancer. My mom had a very bad type of cancer. The type of cancer that causes everyone to shake their head back and forth with a very grim look on their face, that type of cancer. My dad was a wreck and both of my brothers were out of state. I suddenly became the point person for communication, logistics, decisions, and everything else. I called the immediate family and then I called Gretchen. She had to work until 6:00 p.m. but then she would hop in her car and drive the two-hour distance to be with me. I told her I would be fine and she didn't need to do that. She said, "I'm coming. It's not a request but a promise. Do what you have to do today knowing that I'll be there tonight and we can talk about all of it." It was settled. She was coming.

The events of that day are blurred and yet so poignant in my mind. I finally returned home and Gretchen was there, just like she had promised. My brothers were flying in that night but would not arrive until midnight. Gretchen said that she would stay until my brothers arrived, and then she would head back home to be at work at nine o'clock the next morning. This is friendship. This is mentorship. This is the give and take that I have described. I had been there for her, and now she was going to be there for me.

Four very short months later, my mother lost her battle with cancer and left this earth. I did three very drastic things: I quit my job; I sold everything I owned in my house; and I put my home on the market to sell. Everyone thought I was flipping out and losing it, except for one person. Gretchen. She got it, she understood what I was doing. I was changing my life. I had a whole new understanding for how short life is and I did not want to waste another day.

Many, many people tried to tell me about the "first year of grief." But they were forgetting that I had already lived through a "first year of grief" and doing it again was not something I was willing to consider. Gretchen and I talked often. She was encouraging and supportive during this season of transition. I spent many weekends at her home near the beach. Grief. This is what it looks like sometimes.

I spent a year traveling and seeing the world. Apparently it is very common for people who are grieving to travel. I met many of them along my journey. When I returned to the United States I moved to a different state and completely changed careers. Gretchen was a vast source of inspiration and encouragement during this time. She kept reminding me that I could do it. She had done it, and so could I.

This past summer, Gretchen came for my wedding. She was my right-hand gal. We celebrated, as both of our lives were so different from when we first became friends. But we both would tell you that we are grateful. We are grateful for each other, grateful that we did not have to go through these life lessons alone.

Grief and gratitude often travel together. Having a friend who helps you naturally balance the two is a treasure and a find. Is there someone in your world that you could help? Maybe there is a woman in your circle of influence who needs your smile and kind words. Look around. When I first invested in Gretchen after her father passed away I had no idea all the peaks and valleys that our friendship was going to travel through. But those lip glosses and chocolate bandages sure did do the trick. I challenge you to find a woman in your world that needs a chocolate bandage, and then give it to her and see where it goes from there.

Chapter 10

Fast Friends Felicity and Faith

What pops into your mind when you hear the word fast? Race cars are fast, missiles are fast, but are people fast? When I hear the word fast I think of the word instantaneous. It happens in an instant. Blink of an eye, snap of the fingers. Fast is quicker than normal. Normally it takes encountering someone a few times before you realize that you would like to know her more deeply. But on rare occasions it happens instantly.

Sometimes friendships are searched out and sometimes friendships are sudden discoveries. Felicity and Faith were two friends that were found upon our first meeting. I had been moving around a lot but finally resettled in the Pacific Northwest. For weeks I had been looking for a job, and finally secured one. On the first day of my new job, I had a new employee orientation. After the paperwork was done, the HR director took me around the building to meet some of the staff. I was trying to make connections between names and faces but failing miserably.

As we walked down one hallway, I was taken into an office and introduced to Felicity. Immediately I knew we would be friends. I do not know how to explain it, but I just knew. We chatted a little bit about her job. She was instrumental in designing the webpage for the company. I thanked her for her excellent work, as I had spent many hours on those pages preparing for my job interview. But it was time for us to move on to the next office so we said a quick farewell. In the next office was a lovely tall woman who was dressed very fashionably. I am tall and many of my friends over the years have not been tall, so I took notice. We introduced ourselves, her name was Faith. Again we had to keep moving, so I said goodbye. We left her office and continued to meet other people throughout the building. But Faith and Felicity were the faces and names that stuck in my head.

As the days went by we got to know each other a little bit more. The three of us would take lunch breaks together and they would take turns stopping by my office to see how the job was going. Many years ago I learned how to "invade" people's lives without it feeling like an invasion. I began this process on Felicity and Faith, as they had been friends for several years. I had never invaded a duo before. In the past my invasions had been one-on-one encounters. This was going to be an interesting challenge.

My schedule was more flexible than theirs, and so I began watching the ebb and flow of their schedules to see how I could fit into it. That is the key to an excellent invasion: fitting myself into her life and her schedule. I know I have done it well when she says things like, "I feel like we have always been friends. When did we even start hanging out?" I sent a calendar request to have a late lunch on a Thursday. This worked with all three of our schedules and our friendships began to blossom over a hot basket of tortilla chips and salsa.

There was an instant familiarity among us. We laughed, talked, and shared on many different levels. Usually more time is needed to develop this depth of friendship. I was hungry for female friendship. Faith and Felicity were enjoying adding a new flavor to their friendship.

Once I have established a loose meeting pattern—meeting for coffee once a week or having lunch every few weeks—then it is time to take the invasion of friendship to the next level. Phase two of the invasion process is spending time together outside of where we normally meet. So for example, Faith, Felicity, and I met at work and spent our time around work. Phase two was finding ways to connect with them outside of work. This could be at our homes, on an outing, or at a specific function.

Faith was single as was I, and her schedule was more flexible than Felicity's. Faith and I kept trying to meet to go shopping because she had such fabulous taste in clothes, but the trips had to be cancelled for various and assorted reasons. Then Faith invited me to a concert and I immediately said yes. A concert would be a great way to connect. The funny part of that situation was that I had met a guy (who later became my husband) and he came to the concert as well. I wanted Faith's opinion about him. I hadn't known Faith for long but I already knew to value her opinion. She gave him a glowing review.

Felicity was a bit harder to track down. She was married and had a very involved family. I had to be satisfied with one-on-one lunches until our schedules became more aligned. It is funny how life works sometimes: the first time Felicity and I spent time together outside of work was a double date. I wanted her opinion, as well, about my new guy.

This question is often asked, "Do you tell her she is being invaded?" It depends on the person and the relationship. If I think she can handle it, then I tell her. If I think she might be intimidated or put off then I do not tell her. Faith and Felicity could handle it. I think by our second lunch I had told them my plan. They were a little surprised but pleased, I think.

The third phase is when the friendship becomes second nature, when I know my friend well enough to find a thoughtful gift for her, or she tells me about an incident accompanied with a statement like, "I absolutely thought of you while it was happening." Felicity, Faith, and I have an excellent example of this. It was during my friendship with them that I became engaged. I had lost my mom and dad several years before and it was really important to Faith and Felicity that I have a bachelorette party and celebrate!

Schedules were tight and funds were low, so the three of us went to a Mexican restaurant for dinner (of course). I love Mexican food and our first lunch as friends had been Mexican food. Together they had created a scavenger hunt for us, well me, to accomplish throughout the evening. Silly things were on the list like asking a stranger to practice walking down the aisle with me, or asking someone to contribute a dollar to my wedding fund. But the best thing of all was ending our evening at an amazing dessert place. I love chocolate and this place served anything and everything chocolate. We laughed, we cried because we laughed so hard, and we ate. It was an evening I will never forget.

Our friendship was fast but so lovely. That is the beauty of developing female friends. Some take years to develop where others take only minutes. Regardless of how quickly or slowly you become friends, everyone will benefit from the experience. There are days that I think about how, if I had not changed everything in my life and picked up and moved, I never would have met Faith and Felicity. I cannot imagine my life here in the Pacific Northwest without them.

Chapter 11

Lover of Souls Sophie

How do we love one person more than another? Why do some people always see the good and others always see the bad? I have been blessed with friendships of both types. Soul-loving Sophie always saw the best in people, even when they were really rotten.

When it comes to people, Sophie is always seeing "the glass half full." I have always enjoyed people and the differences between them, but Sophie brought that enjoyment to an intimate level.

Sophie and I became friends through work. I was working the front desk and she came in looking for a job. We practically hired her on the spot. She had just moved to the area, where she and her boyfriend wanted to get to know one another better. She was actually living with his parents while he rented an apartment with some guys. Sophie and I hit it off right away; I knew her boyfriend, and offered to have coffee with her sometime because she did not have any friends yet.

Getting to know a new friend can feel simple or feel like work depending on the circumstances. Getting to know

Sophie was simple. We saw each other every day as I sat at the front desk and she had to walk through to clock in. We would talk about school, her new life, and the interesting issues of living with her boyfriend's parents. We became loyal friends through this time—sharing the daily things of life does that. I answered the phone the day she called to let the office know she would not be in to work because she was at the beach receiving her boyfriend's proposal. I was there to see her ring when she came back in to work.

Sophie had so much energy and life about her, I always wanted to find a cause and fight for it after we had spent the afternoon together. She was so inspiring, and yet we were drastically different. Sophie and I would laugh all the time about the fact that we never would have been friends in high school. When Sophie was in high school she had been a loner, gothic, and incredibly artistic. I had been very straight-laced, group oriented, and concentrated on my grades as I knew I wanted to go to a four-year university.

It was our differences that made our friendship unique. Sophie often helped me see other people's perspectives. But the main things Sophie offered our friendship was her faith in and love for people. Whenever I think of Sophie I can hear her saying, "but she is such an amazing person." It didn't matter whom we were talking about, this statement would consistently pour out of her mouth.

As I mentioned before, she was incredibly loyal. Sophie thrived on deep-level friendship, which I did as well. Our conversations always pulled a great deal out of each of us. It was amazing to sit down to have a simple "catch up" conversation only to realize why I couldn't let the anger go towards this friend of mine or why I was feeling burnt out at work. We gave each other courage in these unique ways.

I had just begun to paint. I didn't feel that I was very good at it. Sophie had always painted. Paint flowed through her veins. One summer I went to New York to visit some family and tour the city. When I arrived back home there were two huge paintings waiting for me. Sophie and another friend had painted them for me. Later Sophie explained that they wanted to express their belief in me as a woman but also demonstrate my faith through the paintings. I hung these paintings on my wall and used them to inspire myself for years to come. Often I would timidly show Sophie my art projects and she always had admiration for them and incredibly insightful comments.

As our friendship grew we would paint things for each other. Many years later Sophie told me that she is very private with her art and very rarely gives it away. Yet here I had several pieces.

Solid, faithful friendships with women help us see our beauty, our strength, and our value. God designed us to need words and often the men in our lives just do not have enough for us, but our female relationships can help balance us.

Friendship with Sophie held a lovely surprise each time we met. We since have moved far apart from each other but on the rare opportunity that we do get to visit, it is as if no time has passed at all. The years we spent together had a strong impact on us both.

I always want to repeat a good thing. So if I had a friendship that was fun and thought provoking but that person moved away, I would look for another friend that could fill the gap. Through my friendship with Sophie I learned that was terrible thinking. We are all unique and lovely. No one person can take the place of another. There can be similarities, but not replacements. Our friendship also taught me that sometimes having someone drastically different from yourself as your friend can bring much more into your life than someone who is similar to you in ideas and thought.

Over the years, I have discovered that painting really helps me process life. Often I do not know what I want to paint or how I want a painting to look but I know the emotions that I am feeling. Sophie continues to inspire me even though she is far away.

Prayer has been a huge part of my friendship with Sophie. As the years went by, our lives changed in dramatic ways. Prayer with friends allows you to uphold them when they cannot uphold themselves. Sophie and her husband were looking forward to having children. Several years went by and, for whatever reason, a pregnancy did not happen. I truly believed that Sophie and her husband were meant to have a child. I prayed steadily for them as they continued to live their lives and pursue their other dreams. Often Sophie would call discouraged or saddened that yet another month had passed and she was still without child. We would talk and pray. We would hang up, and I would pray some more.

Several years ago, God answered all of those prayers. A little boy was born to Sophie and her husband, and he is the delight of all. They are enjoying this little guy so much.

As you can guess, Sophie was praying for something for me as well. I wanted to be married. I had always dreamed that it would come. Looking back, those were my desert years of singleness. Sophie believed so strongly in her heart that God had someone for me, and in His time and in His way we would find each other. As faithfully as I held up my prayer for her and a future son, Sophie held up for me the prayer of a future husband. God is faithful and He answered our request. It was many years later, but it was answered.

This last year Sophie honored a very unusual request. I asked her to come and paint during my wedding ceremony. I wanted her art and prayers to be a part of my wedding. My sweetly shy Sophie agreed and painted a lovely piece for my new husband and me. The art of that day hangs in our living room and is a constant reminder that God does answer prayer. He does listen to the requests of friends. Those prayers do matter.

One of my favorite episodes in the Bible is the faithfulness of friends. There was a man who was a paraplegic. He wanted to meet Jesus and be healed. Because of his condition he was not able to walk. Four of his friends decided that they would carry him to Jesus. Only once they got to where Jesus was teaching, the building was full, even the sidewalks outside were full. These faithful friends were so close, they were not about to give up. The four friends climbed and carried their friend up to the roof. Together the four tore back the roof, and using some ropes they lowered their friend down right in front of Jesus. They believed that God had a plan for their friend and they were going to do whatever they could to assist their friend. Jesus did heal the man and said that it was the faith of his friends that brought him healing.[4] I want to be a friend like that, and I want to have friends like that. Sophie, who loves souls so much, was and is this kind of friend for me.

---

[4] Mark 2:1-12.

Chapter 12

Mentoring Towards God, Towards Hope

Let's return to the story of Mary and Elizabeth. The Bible tells us that Mary stayed with Elizabeth and mute Zechariah for three months and then returned home.[5] This is a beautiful story of friendship and mentorship. Mary had just been given very shocking news and the angel knew that she was going to need guidance and companionship to get through it all well. God preordained Elizabeth to be six months pregnant before Mary was chosen. I believe that each of us have some preordained relationships in our lives. Are we seeing them? Are we paying attention?

I have shared how my mother was the first to teach me about mentorship. Your family is preordained. Iris and Addie were divinely placed in my life when my brothers chose to marry them. Could I learn something from them? Absolutely. Pam and Wendy were carefully sought out for the very specific reasons of wisdom. Tracy sought me out through work. Mira

---

[5]   Gospel of Luke 1:56.

and Sophie crossed my path at the workplace. Vivian blessed me by being an authentic roommate. And Gretchen, Faith, and Felicity were invaded because they were worth knowing.

Mentoring relationships have brought me security, truth, and tremendous personal growth. Just start with one woman. Where do you spend your time? If you are at church, look for a woman at church. If you go to the gym regularly, look at the gym. Maybe you have small children, then find a women who has children five years older than yours—just that mom's composure will give you hope. Maybe you love your job and work many hours a day. Find a woman at work that you admire and ask her to lunch. Everyone has to take a lunch, right?

As you get more comfortable becoming friends with women, venture out of your comfort zone. Find a woman that has a life incredibly different than yours. For many years I was single and I purposely chose to be friends with women who were married and had kids. We often could help each other see the benefits of the life we were living by seeing it through the other person's eyes.

At the beginning of the book, the question was posed: Is mentoring truly an extraordinary experience?

My answer to this is yes, it is. It is extraordinary to mentor another woman, and it is an extraordinary experience to be mentored by another woman.

I would like to share a practical thought with you. I strive to have five solid female relationships in my life at all times. I chose five because I have five fingers on one hand. I had read articles about how having just one friend can be unhealthy and isolating. But I had personally experienced that having

The Many Facets of a Woman

too many intimate friends can be exhausting. I kept thinking to myself, "I want to count on one hand the important women in my life." Thus the number five was chosen.

A short story to illustrate the value of having a fabulous five: A devastating event occurred one Saturday. My heart was breaking in two and I knew I needed prayer and truthful words quickly. It was around nine o'clock in the morning. I had five names to choose from. I chose Wendy. The phone rang and rang, but I was sent to voice mail. I left a short cryptic message ending with, "Please call me soon." I went to the next woman but the same thing happened: no answer, only voice mail. This happens sometimes. We all have busy, hectic lives and as much as we want to be there for our friends all the time, it just isn't possible. That is why I try to have five women, so that no one person feels overwhelmed or smothered. And I am not put out or left hanging if one of them is busy with her life. Interestingly enough, the five women do not normally know each other. But back to the story.

I called the third woman and she picked up. We talked through what happened and she caught my tears through the telephone and then she prayed with me. We hung up. I felt whole again and ready to face the day. As I was cleaning up the kitchen and going about my normal Saturday morning tasks, Wendy called back. I will never forget what she said, "Was I the first one? You called me first and I wasn't able to answer?" I told her that was true, she had been my first call. Her response was this: "I knew it, as soon as I saw that you called and the time stamp. I told my husband that you had called me first but went to the next person on your list. I'm sorry I missed your call, I'm here now and I want to listen." She was so genuine in her disappointment in missing the call, I had to smile. We both knew it was not a contest but as Wendy said later, "It's just the principle of the thing. You called me first, I wanted to be the first one to pray for you and to listen."

Find your five women, or three women, or eight women. Begin discovering the many facets of your womanhood. Be willing to share who you are with others. Be willing to be shaped by others. It will bless them and it will bless you. And your life will never be the same, it will only be better and blessed.

You and I were created in the image of God. That cry of the heart "I was trying to be you" is ingrained in us, but with a twist. Our cry is actually to be like God. We long for His image to be evident within us. I learned so much from each of these women because they were striving to be more like the divinely created piece of God that we each are.

God looks at my soul the way that Sophie looks at souls. He sees the potential, the good, and the beauty that only I, as a child of God, can hold.

When we are calling out to the Lord, He is fast and friendly in responding. He wants a relationship with each one of us, His beloved. Faith and Felicity remind me of this truth every day.

God knows the grief and gratitude that is going to ripple through our lives. He wants to walk along with us, in our midst. So often I think I need to get to a healthier place before I call to God. This is absurd thinking. God wants to meet me

The Many Facets of a Woman

in my brokenness. He wants to help hold my grief and lead me to gratitude just as Gretchen and I did for each other.

Prayer changes things, as I have tried to illustrate. But having a friend who consistently reminds me of the faithfulness of God leads me to take prayer seriously and respect its power, which in turn reminds me I am serving the Living God!

As I read and study the Bible I am reminded of the fact that God often chooses very private moments to talk to his children, His image bearers. Precisely Private Vivian taught me this. She demonstrated for me how utterly personal and private our God can be—that some things really are just between God and me, no one else.

In the book of James, the author describes a man looking at a mirror and seeing himself for who he really is. But as soon as the man walks away he forgets the image that he saw.[6] Having a friend who mirrors my every emotion definitely helps me to see myself for who I really am. I am my own worst critic. For the past several years I have prayed that God would help me to see myself the way that others see me. Mirror Mira provided this opportunity for me. Often the qualities I admired in her were qualities I also possessed but was unable to see. For example, being welcoming and passionate engages people in friendliness and kindness. Having Mira as my mirror has given me confidence to be who I am and to focus on the strengths of my personality and have a positive perspective on myself.

As I read the pages of the Bible, it is clear our God loves a great adventure! He enjoys the thrill of something new.

---

[6] James 1:22-24

Adventuresome Addie reminds me that there is still so much of life to live, and I need to be and act as the leading lady in my own life. Each day is a new adventure, but I must go looking for those adventures.

As the years have gone by I believe that I have cultivated the art of inviting. Often people say that I make them feel welcome. This is not a natural trait for me. But I have had so many years of Iris inviting me into her world that I have managed to soak in a bit of her sunshine. I want more. I want to be more inviting. I want to be more thoughtful of others. I want to be more like Iris but in my own way, with my own twist. I want to be like our God who endlessly is inviting me in, inviting me back to fellowship with Him, inviting me into a deeper, richer life.

One of Thought-Full Tracy's greatest and most frequently displayed gifts was her familiarity with Scripture. She would write it on cards and give them to anyone and everyone. We would cross paths in the hallway, and in a very quick and concise way she would share what God had opened her eyes to that morning in her daily Bible reading. The Bible was so real to her and so valued. Just by spending a few minutes with her I knew she had many full thoughts about Scripture. I remember one day so clearly. Tracy had just shared an insight from Scripture and was walking away from me. I remember thinking, "I want that. I want to become an older, wiser woman who LOVES the Scriptures." At that moment God profoundly impressed on my heart that the way to do that was one day at a time. The same way Tracy had. Tracy had purposed to keep her mind full of thoughts about Scripture. I could do this. I could mimic this trait. I could further discover the image of God in me by keeping my mind full of thoughts of Him, the One who cannot stop thinking of me.[7] Yes, I have done this and continue to do so daily.

Parenting is still something ahead of me, yet to do. I had nine amazing months to practice when two little boys tripped into my life. They exited as quickly as they had entered. I look towards the day when parenting is a daily occurrence for me once again. God taught me so much about Himself in those brief months of being a parent. In the deepest place of my soul He taught me that He loves me unconditionally. No matter how terribly I behave or how many temper tantrums I have, He is waiting to love me. Period. Love. Unconditional. Always. I want to be a parent like Pam. I want to raise my children in a way that will grow them stronger to face the challenges of life. I hold her model in my heart. It is tucked in tightly next to hope. Hope for brighter days, hope for a treasured child of my own. Each day that passes and the request remains unfulfilled, I am reminded of Petee and Pam. I can choose to obey God and be faithful to the many other things that are before me, and make the hope stronger. Or, I can choose to not listen, turn away from God, from hope, and suffer the consequence of hopelessness.

Friend, Sister, if you feel trapped in hopelessness there is a way out. Find another sister to pray for you. Find one small thing to hope in. Talk to God. Believe that our Father is a Father of hope. Then don't look back. Choose each day to cultivate the smallest amount of hope. If you can do this, then I promise you the hope will grow. It might take days, it might

---

[7] Psalms 139:17

take years, it might take a very long time. But God promises hope. I know, I have been there. I have walked this path.

My amazingly strong mother died of cancer. I watched it happen, helpless. This woman that had been my pillar of strength for 37 years was ravaged by a disease that is no respecter of persons. Cancer doesn't care if you are rich or poor, young or old. It wants to devour its victim.

Mother's Day of that year was sad. I was sad because I missed my boys. I was sad because I was going to miss my mom. On that bright sunny Sunday I sat with my mother and we bawled our eyes out. We both knew this was her last Mother's Day. She was not going to make it to the next one. We began to grieve the loss. The loss of my dearest and closest friend. There is one blessing in cancer. Only one. It gives you time. My mom and I had time to say all the things we wanted to say to each other. We cried much. We had spent years laughing but now it was a season of tears. We washed ourselves in those tears. The hopelessness was brewing.

One week before my mother passed away, my father was rushed to the emergency room. He was diagnosed with a cancerous brain tumor. Stage IV. Not good. The hopelessness was beginning to boil. The world as I knew it was crumbling all around me. I will never forget that day in the hospital when the doctor came out and said almost verbatim what another doctor had said four months previously, "Your father has cancer; we removed what we could, but it doesn't look good."

Hopelessness engulfed me. I clung to the end of the lifeline, the knowledge that God loves me unconditionally and that He is good. As I sobbed in my brothers' arms in the hospital waiting room I remember thinking, "God, I know there is grace in the midst of this horrific storm, but I don't know where it is."

All the steadfastness that Diana Smith had modeled for me had been used up. I used it up caring for her. Now my brothers and I had to care for my dad? Black, thick hopelessness. Eleven weeks and one day separate the physical deaths of my parents. Most days the hopelessness was all around me but my women, my sisters-in-Christ, would reach in and uphold me. They upheld me through prayer, cards, facials, words, and silence.

"God, I know there is grace in the midst of this, but I don't know where it is." Some days this was all I could pray. A strand of a rope, but I hung on. Some days my sisters-in-faith held onto me and held onto my rope for me.

Hold onto hope. It will grow, I promise. It will overtake the hopelessness in time. Several months later—I don't know when, I don't know how—God showed me the grace in the midst of this terrible situation.

The grace was this: TIME. Somewhere along the path of my dad's illness one of the doctors explained to us that if my dad had not had the 911 episode, and if they had not discovered the tumor that night, he would have died before my mom. Read that sentence again—my dad would have suddenly died, without any explanation, before my mom.

God gave us time. He gave us eleven extra weeks and one extra day with my dad. The tumor affected my dad's speech, his vision, his hearing, his dexterity, but not his disposition. To my dad's dying day he was jolly, comical, and the best patient we could ask for.

It wasn't until the hopelessness was less and the hope was greater that I was able to see the grace. But it was there, all along. God with His abundant grace was right there with me.

I tell you all of this as a testimony of the influence of a woman's life upon me. My mom instilled in me strength and steadfastness. I never would have made it through that season without her continual investing in me and consistent modeling of true strength and determination.

Be a woman who encourages another woman. Invade her life and introduce a trait into her life that she desperately needs. She may not even know she needs it, but God does. God knows you intimately. God knows her intimately. Discover the many facets of our God together.

Made in the USA
Lexington, KY
26 February 2017